PERFECT PLANNING

4 *Life!*

A Workbook for the Art of Time Management,
Setting Your Goals, and Achieving Your True Potential

TINA RUSSEK

Motivational Speaker, Designer/Artist, and Professional Organizer

PAGE PUBLISHING, INC.
Conneaut Lake, PA

First originally published by Page Publishing 2021

ISBN 978-1-6624-3698-7 (hc)
ISBN 978-1-6624-3697-0 (digital)

Printed in the United States of America

First of all, I want to give God all the glory for His direction, inspiration, and miracles in writing this book. I pray that His blessings and His guidance will bring clarity and joy to everyone that reads this book.

I dedicate this workbook to the people that inspired me, supported, and believed in all my dreams.

My mother, Evelyn, who was amazed at my talent, tenacity, and great attitude about life. She would say when I was a little girl, "I always looked forward to seeing the next day." Thank you for your integrity, love, and faith.

My brother, Richard, you're one of my best friends, and we have always had the same sense of humor; you've been my biggest fan, rooting me on with all my projects.

My auntie Rosie—elegant, beautiful, kind, and shared her positive philosophy with me. She had a remarkable way of making everyone feel so appreciated. She dressed beautifully and was my first fashion icon.

Thank you for being there for me.

The greatest discovery of any generation is that human beings can alter their lives by altering the attitudes of their minds.

—Albert Schweitzer

*M*any of life's failures are people who did not realize how close they were to success when they gave up.

—Thomas A. Edison

Contents

*S*pecial thanks to KC Enzer, who introduced me to a sales-and-goal-setting program called "The Master Mind" created and written by the late, great, Dale Carnegie and Napoleon Hill.

KC also made invaluable suggestions that helped me in defining the eight categories, which are the foundation of this book.

In creating this workbook, I was inspired by the original program of Mastermind to assist you, my dear reader, to break down and accomplish all your goals and projects from year to year, in the hopes that you will achieve your greatest dreams.

Thank you.

Tina Russek was born with the organizational gene! When she was just five years old, she created filing systems for all her animal drawings. Her parents taught her the value of a dollar and the concept of keeping things in good repair. Tina's passion grew along with her God-given gift of organization and managing one's life so effectively.

Tina's bedroom as a teen and her home now as an adult is one with efficiency and order. Nothing is out of place. "Everything has a home and must be returned to its proper place after being used" is her own favorite quote. When people visit, they are struck by the "structure" of how she lives. Her gifts have been put to good use. Her unique system, which she developed, has been perfected over the years.

Several years ago, Tina embarked on a "mastermind program," whereby she and a friend would hold each other accountable for their plans and dreams for each other's life. This program worked so well that Tina knew it was to be the main component necessary to shape her philosophy of Perfect Planning 4 Life: Life organization at its finest! This program is a process that she has professionally utilized her entire life. Tina is now anxious and ready to start helping others through the Perfect Planning 4 Life program.

The concept of Perfect Planning 4 Life: Your future dreams are outlined in daily, weekly, monthly, and yearly categories. So much can be accomplished when you plan your daily, weekly, monthly, and yearly goals. Imagine how great an organized life could be for you and your family with Perfect Planning 4 Life!

If you have ever thought or dreamed of organizing your life simply and effectively, you must subscribe to Tina's system of a Perfect Planning 4 Life.

There is nothing stronger than the testimony of satisfied clients. Many lives have been transformed by their daily observations and applying Tina's system to everyday life…and then watching their own magic transformation materialize!

There is a fountain of youth: it is your mind, your talents, the creativity you bring to your life and the lives of people you love. When you learn to tap this source, you will truly have defeated age.

—Sophia Loren

Dreams are only dreams until you put a date
on them and then they become a goal.
Goals direct your life!

*L*ive each day as if your life had just begun.

—Johann Wolfgang von Goethe

*L*ife has two rules:
No. 1: Never quit.
No. 2: Always remember rule no. 1.

—Unknown

$\mathcal{Y}$ou are never too old to become what you might have been.

—Sally Field

Thank you, Sally!

What is perfect planning for life?

An obstacle is often a stepping stone.

—Prescott

*G*ood question. Let me explain…

Perfect Planning 4 Life is *the* definitive goal setting and time management program. It is the only tool you will ever need to organize your thoughts, desires, and ambitions on a daily basis, and all contained in a useful workbook that you personally customize and maintain.

Everyone has twenty-four hours in the day, so how do you get the most out of your day, your week, your month, and your year?

(Hint: It starts with breaking down your thoughts, desires, and ambitions into manageable increments.)

First, your *road map of life* needs to be identified and defined into categories that get you where you want to go. I believe mostly everything can be achieved with eight master categories created for your journey, and when these specific categories are defined and outlined, you can create a road map to your *future* by an orderly and well-defined *present*.

What are the master categories? Okay…let me share these eight fundamentals:

- *Home.* Because that's where we reside and regenerate. Because that's where our heart is, because Dorothy got it right: There's no place like home, and we need to honor the place where we live.
- *Health.* Because you can't buy it, and you can't take it for granted. And it can be maintained with a little effort.
- *Finances.* Because respect for yourself starts with respect for the provision God has given you. Get your finances under control, and find freedom you have never before experienced.
- *Spiritual.* Because unless the soul is nurtured, the mind and body cannot follow. If your path is made straight, God can be invited on the trip called your life.
- *Friends and family.* Because a journey without them isn't a journey worth taking.
- *Business.* Because as scary a category as this might be to some and as challenging as this might be to others, this category can and will become as exciting as you can imagine. And imagination is the key to good business, resulting in great success!
- *Personal and Fun.* Because we tend to forget to play and to take care of ourselves when we get all "grown" up and serious. We need to remember to take our adult crayons and color our hair, color our toes, and color our life!
- *"Free" category.* Because you may need to address something special. Something that may take "moving on" from being stuck, or "courage" to start. Something that every day you might be able to take daily small steps to conquer so that, maybe in one year on this program, something good gets a little bit better, or maybe something bad gets gone for good!

$\mathcal{E}$ither you run the day…or the day runs you.

—Jim Ralm

What are the tools needed to work these categories into life-changing events?
(Hint: Pencil and paper…or iPad. Your call.)

Writing down your goals in each category. These can consist of home improvement, losing weight, making more money, getting a degree, traveling, finding the right man or women, volunteering, saving for something important, reconnecting with old friends. It's all up to you. Perhaps completing your bucket list…or just improving your life.

Making a conscious decision of what you want. *What do you want to accomplish? Who do you wish to become? What dream do you want to see become a reality?* The minute you define it and put a "deadline" or completion date on it, it becomes a goal and no longer just a dream. You put power to it and permission for yourself to go for it!

Partnering in this Perfect Planning 4 Life workbook. A partner will keep you accountable on task, support your progress, your accomplishments, and successes. It also gives you an opportunity for that rarest of blessings, benefitting another human being with encouragement, support, and ultimately, trust in each other's well-being.

This program and workbook is designed to be reviewed and then replaced every year with new goals, new desires, and new places in the heart yet uncovered, just waiting to be revealed to you! It is said if we stop learning, stop reaching, stop searching, we stop living. I planned a Perfect Planning 4 Life so you may live, and live well and happy as you travel through the years.

May God bless you on your journey. I wish you great accomplishments through true direction, resulting in immeasurable joy.

If you have any questions, please visit my website at **www.perfectplanning4life.com.**

Personal Affirmations

*S*adly, common knowledge and common
courtesy are no longer common…

—Tina Russek

*T*aking the high road is always the best road.

—Tina Russek

$\mathcal{B}$egin each affirmation with "I, (your name), am healthy, aware, successful, happy, etc."

1 _____

2 _____

3 _____

4 _____

5 _____

6 _____

7 _____

8 _____

9 _____

10 _____

11 _____

12 _____

13 _____

14 _____

15 _____

16 _____

17 _____

18 _____

19 _____

20 _____

Speak these to yourself every day!

Fifty-Two Week Goal Planning Overview

Eighty percent of life is showing up.

—Woody Allen

Football is like life—it requires perseverance, self-denial, hard work, sacrifice, dedication, and respect for authority.

—Vince Lombardi

Overview of year:

1. What are your greatest goals?_____
2. What are you looking forward to?_____
3. What do you appreciate this year?_____

Most important goals for categories:

1. Home._____
2. Health._____
3. Personal and fun._____
4. Spiritual._____
5. Finances._____
6. Friends and family._____
7. Business._____
8. Moving On and Balance._____
9. "Free" category._____

Try using one word. Just say what your heart says!

This is Your Book

$\mathcal{Y}$es, this is your book. It is a tool that you should try and use every day. This book is to be used, written in, thought upon, and stylized just for you.

Here are the guidelines for you to apply and hopefully enjoy.

1. *Use the book every day.* Check what you have accomplished (I like to highlight each item out). Open up your workbook and check it every day to record what you have completed. However; if you stay "present" and pay attention to your spending, your eating, your personal production, you will start to see and feel a new sense of accomplishment and direction.

2. *Keeping a partner accountable is huge!* It is also a source of feedback and encouragement; you and your partner should celebrate your successes and address what is not completed and why. Yes, you need to hear that and look at what you are avoiding and why. This is how we grow.

3. *I have written this workbook so it will work with you!* Take notes! Write your heart out! Share it with someone you trust, and don't be afraid of making mistakes. That's okay.

4. *When writing out the master categories at the beginning of your workbook, stick to five goals per category.* You may add to that original number year to year. I think five items per category is doable and not too overwhelming.

5. *The key to success is consistency.* It's amazing what we accomplish by just doing a little every day. Whether it's walking a mile, taking the steps instead of the elevator, cutting out sugar once a week, or writing down a goal and breaking it down in a step-by-step procedure, you will eventually accomplish an extraordinary amount of goals.

6. *Mixing goals and chores.* Perfect Planning 4 Life! is life. We have big goals, little goals, and everyday chores, errands, and "to-do" stuffs. That should be included in your fifty-two-week section of the workbook. Yes! It's a combination of everything you want to accomplish that week. I feel that it is important to chip away at the mountain of daily work and play (yes, you need to play!). Combining the *goals and the routine of life* is a good balance. When you combine your daily task and yearly goals you will be amazed at what you will accomplish.

   Good balance. When you do that combining of "tasks," you will see that you accomplish more.

7. *Make this* Your *Journey.* Indeed, the journey of a thousand miles starts with one step, and I hope and pray that all my readers and believers will start with this; your first step.
   - Write down your affirmations.
   - Write down your innermost thoughts, and plan for new successes in life.
   - Don't give up. Celebrate your accomplishments and enjoy your journey.

                              and

   - Start where you are,
   - Use what you have, and
   - Do what you can.

May you be blessed along the way.

The only thing worse than being blind
is having sight but no vision.

—Helen Keller

Categories for the Year

$\mathcal{M}$aster Goals for the (year) _____

A—Home

1 _____
2 _____
3 _____
4 _____
5 _____

B—Health

1 _____
2 _____
3 _____
4 _____
5 _____

C—Personal and Fun

1 _____
2 _____
3 _____
4 _____
5 _____

D—Spiritual

1 _____
2 _____
3 _____
4 _____
5 _____

E—Finance

1 _____
2 _____
3 _____
4 _____
5 _____

F—Friends and Family

1 _____
2 _____
3 _____
4 _____
5 _____

G—Business

1 _____
2 _____
3 _____
4 _____
5 _____

H—Moving On

1 _____
2 _____
3 _____
4 _____
5 _____

I- "Free" Category

1 _____
2 _____
3 _____
4 _____
5 _____

Miracles this year

1 _____
2 _____
3 _____
4 _____
5 _____

Challenges this year

1 _____
2 _____
3 _____
4 _____
5 _____

Additional "to do"

1 _____
2 _____
3 _____
4 _____
5 _____

My successes this year

1 _____
2 _____
3 _____
4 _____
5 _____

Notes

1 _____
2 _____
3 _____
4 _____
5 _____

Extra Projects

1 _____
2 _____
3 _____

4 _____
5 _____

We become what we think about.

—Earl Nightingale

I say to everybody, "Love is what wakes you up in the morning, love is what makes you walk, and love is what makes you hope."

—Jerry Lewis

Master Categories

Example Sheet

	Perfect Planning 4 Life Master Categories						
	Categories	Total Count	No. of Most Important	1/4 Yr. Completed	1/2 Yr. Completed	3/4 Yr. Completed	Completed	Percent Completed
A	Home: Repairs, organizing/ remodeling, etc.	5	3	2	3	4	5	100%
B	Health: Doctor appointments, eating right, exercising, losing weight and relaxing	5	3	3	3	4	5	100%
C	Personal: Nails, hair, projects, errands	5	5	2	3	4	5	100%
D	Spiritual: Church/Bible study, volunteering/ prayer time	5	2	1	3	4	4	80%
E	Finance: Managing bills, savings, investing, budgeting	5	3	3	4	4	4	80%
F	Friends: Visiting, writing, reviewing Perfect Planning 4 Life! with your partner	5	5	2	2	4	5	100%

	Categories	Total Count	No. of Most Important	1/4 Yr. Completed	1/2 Yr. Completed	3/4 Yr. Completed	Completed	Percent Completed
G	Business: Work, scheduling hours, projects, reports, and meetings	5	4	2	3	4	4	80%
H	Moving on and Balance: Dating, losing weight, time to be still, time to reflect	5	2	2	2	4	5	100%
I	"Free" Categories: Your final goal that is all yours and nobody else.	5	3	2	3	5	5	100%
	Total:	45	31	19	26	37	42	93%

*R*emember, if it doesn't kill you…
It can always be used for material…

—Tina Russek

*R*emember to always be gracious, even if it kills you.

—Tina Russek

	Categories	Total Count	No. of Most Important	1/4 Yr. Completed	1/2 Yr. Completed	3/4 Yr. Completed	Completed	Percent Completed
	Perfect Planning 4 Life Master Categories							
A	Home: Repairs, organizing/ remodeling, etc.							
B	Health: Doctor appointments, eating right, exercising, losing weight, and relaxing							
C	Personal: Nails, hair, projects, errands							
D	Spiritual: Church/Bible study, volunteering/ prayer time							
E	Finance: Managing bills, savings, investing, budgeting							
F	Friends: Visiting, writing, reviewing Perfect Planning 4 Life! with your partner							

G	Business: Work, scheduling hours, projects, reports, and meetings Moving on and Balance:						
H	Dating, losing weight, time to be still, time to reflect "Free" Categories:						
I	Your final goal that is all yours and nobody else.						

Weekly Goal Sheets

$\mathcal{B}$egin each day as if it were on purpose.

—Will Smith

Weekly Goal Sheet

Week 1   From _____ _____   To _____ _____
                    (Month)   (Day)   (Month)   (Day)

A. Home

1 _____
2 _____
3 _____
4 _____
5 _____

B. Health

1 _____
2 _____
3 _____
4 _____
5 _____

C. Personal and Fun

1 _____
2 _____
3 _____
4 _____
5 _____

D. Spiritual

1 _____
2 _____
3 _____
4 _____
5 _____

E. Finance

1 _____
2 _____
3 _____
4 _____
5 _____

F. Friends and Family

1 _____
2 _____
3 _____
4 _____
5 _____

G. Business

1 _____
2 _____
3 _____
4 _____
5 _____

H. Moving On

1 _____
2 _____
3 _____
4 _____
5 _____

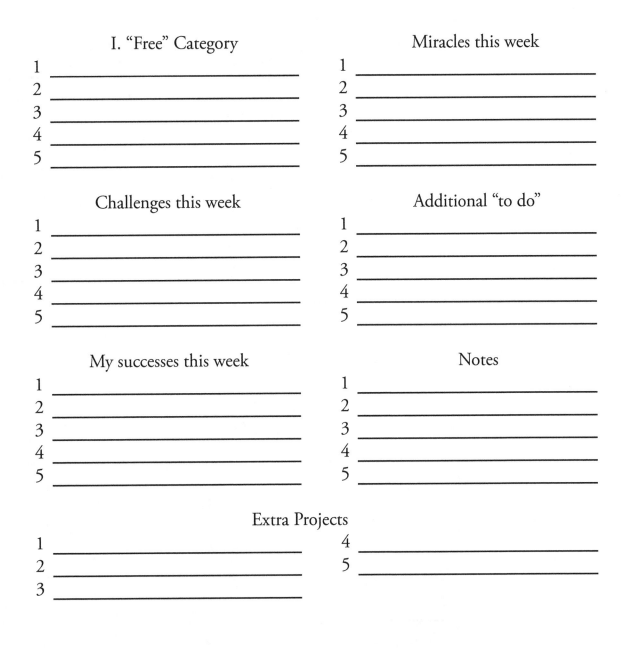

I. "Free" Category

1 _____
2 _____
3 _____
4 _____
5 _____

Miracles this week

1 _____
2 _____
3 _____
4 _____
5 _____

Challenges this week

1 _____
2 _____
3 _____
4 _____
5 _____

Additional "to do"

1 _____
2 _____
3 _____
4 _____
5 _____

My successes this week

1 _____
2 _____
3 _____
4 _____
5 _____

Notes

1 _____
2 _____
3 _____
4 _____
5 _____

Extra Projects

1 _____
2 _____
3 _____

4 _____
5 _____

Week 2 From _____ _____ To _____ _____
(Month)   (Day)   (Month)   (Day)

A. Home

1 _____
2 _____
3 _____
4 _____
5 _____

B. Health

1 _____
2 _____
3 _____
4 _____
5 _____

C. Personal and Fun

1 _____
2 _____
3 _____
4 _____
5 _____

D. Spiritual

1 _____
2 _____
3 _____
4 _____
5 _____

E. Finance

1 _____
2 _____
3 _____
4 _____
5 _____

F. Friends and Family

1 _____
2 _____
3 _____
4 _____
5 _____

G. Business

1 _____
2 _____
3 _____
4 _____
5 _____

H. Moving On

1 _____
2 _____
3 _____
4 _____
5 _____

I. "Free" Category

1 _____
2 _____
3 _____
4 _____
5 _____

Miracles this week

1 _____
2 _____
3 _____
4 _____
5 _____

Challenges this week

1 _____
2 _____
3 _____
4 _____
5 _____

Additional "to do"

1 _____
2 _____
3 _____
4 _____
5 _____

My successes this week

1 _____
2 _____
3 _____
4 _____
5 _____

Notes

1 _____
2 _____
3 _____
4 _____
5 _____

Extra Projects

1 _____
2 _____
3 _____

4 _____
5 _____

Week 3

From
_____ _____
(Month)   (Day)

To
_____ _____
(Month)   (Day)

A. Home

1 _____
2 _____
3 _____
4 _____
5 _____

B. Health

1 _____
2 _____
3 _____
4 _____
5 _____

C. Personal and Fun

1 _____
2 _____
3 _____
4 _____
5 _____

D. Spiritual

1 _____
2 _____
3 _____
4 _____
5 _____

E. Finance

1 _____
2 _____
3 _____
4 _____
5 _____

F. Friends and Family

1 _____
2 _____
3 _____
4 _____
5 _____

G. Business

1 _____
2 _____
3 _____
4 _____
5 _____

H. Moving On

1 _____
2 _____
3 _____
4 _____
5 _____

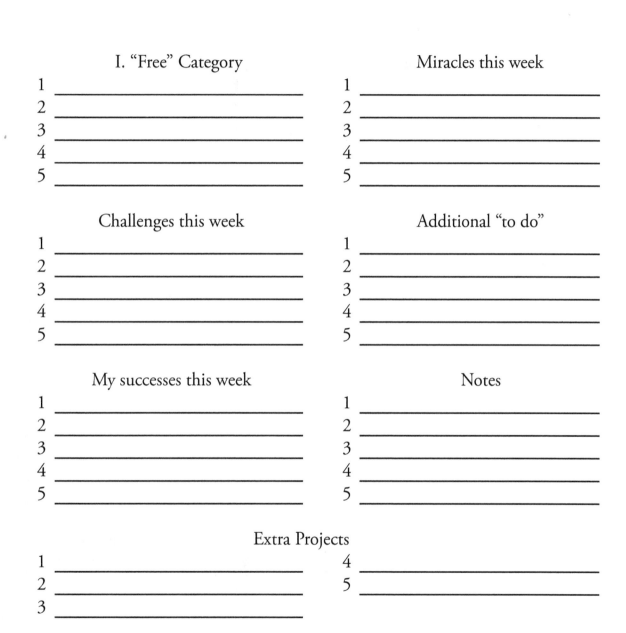

I. "Free" Category

1 _____
2 _____
3 _____
4 _____
5 _____

Miracles this week

1 _____
2 _____
3 _____
4 _____
5 _____

Challenges this week

1 _____
2 _____
3 _____
4 _____
5 _____

Additional "to do"

1 _____
2 _____
3 _____
4 _____
5 _____

My successes this week

1 _____
2 _____
3 _____
4 _____
5 _____

Notes

1 _____
2 _____
3 _____
4 _____
5 _____

Extra Projects

1 _____
2 _____
3 _____

4 _____
5 _____

Week 4 From _____ _____ To _____ _____
                (Month)   (Day)   (Month)   (Day)

A. Home

1 _____
2 _____
3 _____
4 _____
5 _____

B. Health

1 _____
2 _____
3 _____
4 _____
5 _____

C. Personal and Fun

1 _____
2 _____
3 _____
4 _____
5 _____

D. Spiritual

1 _____
2 _____
3 _____
4 _____
5 _____

E. Finance

1 _____
2 _____
3 _____
4 _____
5 _____

F. Friends and Family

1 _____
2 _____
3 _____
4 _____
5 _____

G. Business

1 _____
2 _____
3 _____
4 _____
5 _____

H. Moving On

1 _____
2 _____
3 _____
4 _____
5 _____

I. "Free" Category

1 _____
2 _____
3 _____
4 _____
5 _____

Miracles this week

1 _____
2 _____
3 _____
4 _____
5 _____

Challenges this week

1 _____
2 _____
3 _____
4 _____
5 _____

Additional "to do"

1 _____
2 _____
3 _____
4 _____
5 _____

My successes this week

1 _____
2 _____
3 _____
4 _____
5 _____

Notes

1 _____
2 _____
3 _____
4 _____
5 _____

Extra Projects

1 _____
2 _____
3 _____

4 _____
5 _____

Week 5   From _____ _____   To _____ _____
              (Month)   (Day)   (Month)   (Day)

A. Home

1 _____
2 _____
3 _____
4 _____
5 _____

B. Health

1 _____
2 _____
3 _____
4 _____
5 _____

C. Personal and Fun

1 _____
2 _____
3 _____
4 _____
5 _____

D. Spiritual

1 _____
2 _____
3 _____
4 _____
5 _____

E. Finance

1 _____
2 _____
3 _____
4 _____
5 _____

F. Friends and Family

1 _____
2 _____
3 _____
4 _____
5 _____

G. Business

1 _____
2 _____
3 _____
4 _____
5 _____

H. Moving On

1 _____
2 _____
3 _____
4 _____
5 _____

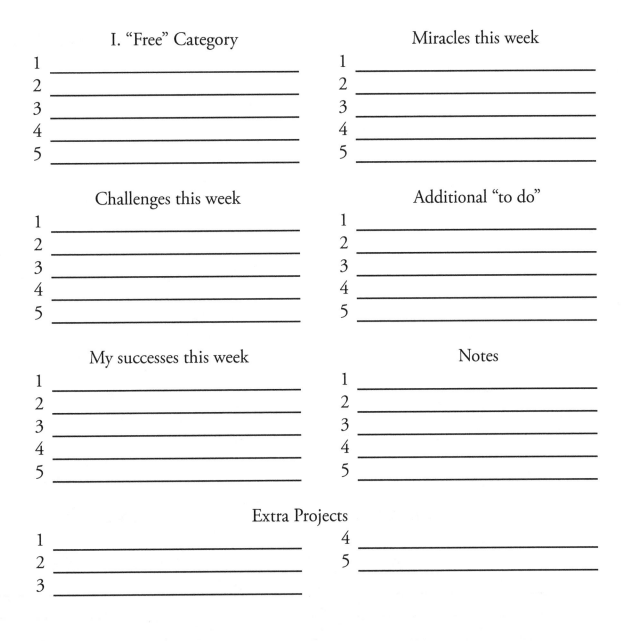

I. "Free" Category

1 _____

2 _____

3 _____

4 _____

5 _____

Miracles this week

1 _____

2 _____

3 _____

4 _____

5 _____

Challenges this week

1 _____

2 _____

3 _____

4 _____

5 _____

Additional "to do"

1 _____

2 _____

3 _____

4 _____

5 _____

My successes this week

1 _____

2 _____

3 _____

4 _____

5 _____

Notes

1 _____

2 _____

3 _____

4 _____

5 _____

Extra Projects

1 _____

2 _____

3 _____

4 _____

5 _____

Week 6   From _____ _____   To _____ _____
                  (Month)   (Day)   (Month)   (Day)

A. Home

1 _____
2 _____
3 _____
4 _____
5 _____

B. Health

1 _____
2 _____
3 _____
4 _____
5 _____

C. Personal and Fun

1 _____
2 _____
3 _____
4 _____
5 _____

D. Spiritual

1 _____
2 _____
3 _____
4 _____
5 _____

E. Finance

1 _____
2 _____
3 _____
4 _____
5 _____

F. Friends and Family

1 _____
2 _____
3 _____
4 _____
5 _____

G. Business

1 _____
2 _____
3 _____
4 _____
5 _____

H. Moving On

1 _____
2 _____
3 _____
4 _____
5 _____

I. "Free" Category

1 _____
2 _____
3 _____
4 _____
5 _____

Miracles this week

1 _____
2 _____
3 _____
4 _____
5 _____

Challenges this week

1 _____
2 _____
3 _____
4 _____
5 _____

Additional "to do"

1 _____
2 _____
3 _____
4 _____
5 _____

My successes this week

1 _____
2 _____
3 _____
4 _____
5 _____

Notes

1 _____
2 _____
3 _____
4 _____
5 _____

Extra Projects

1 _____
2 _____
3 _____

4 _____
5 _____

Week 7

From _____ _____ To _____ _____
        (Month)   (Day)   (Month)   (Day)

A. Home

1 _____
2 _____
3 _____
4 _____
5 _____

B. Health

1 _____
2 _____
3 _____
4 _____
5 _____

C. Personal and Fun

1 _____
2 _____
3 _____
4 _____
5 _____

D. Spiritual

1 _____
2 _____
3 _____
4 _____
5 _____

E. Finance

1 _____
2 _____
3 _____
4 _____
5 _____

F. Friends and Family

1 _____
2 _____
3 _____
4 _____
5 _____

G. Business

1 _____
2 _____
3 _____
4 _____
5 _____

H. Moving On

1 _____
2 _____
3 _____
4 _____
5 _____

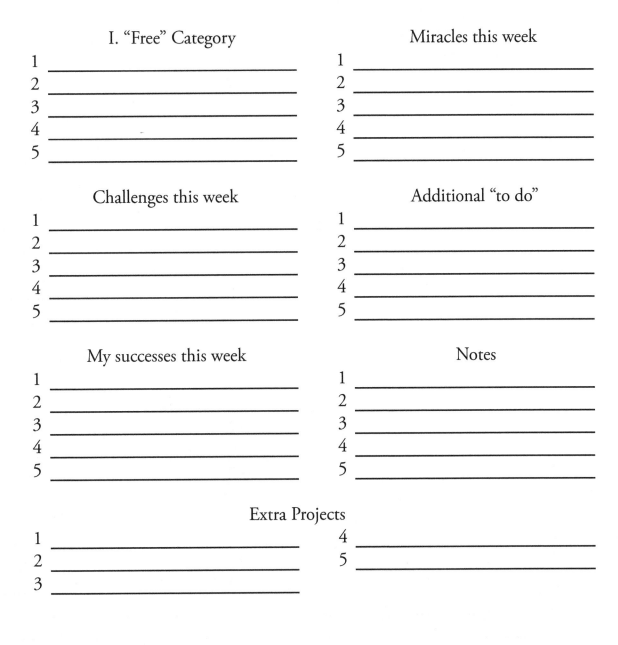

I. "Free" Category

1 _____
2 _____
3 _____
4 _____
5 _____

Miracles this week

1 _____
2 _____
3 _____
4 _____
5 _____

Challenges this week

1 _____
2 _____
3 _____
4 _____
5 _____

Additional "to do"

1 _____
2 _____
3 _____
4 _____
5 _____

My successes this week

1 _____
2 _____
3 _____
4 _____
5 _____

Notes

1 _____
2 _____
3 _____
4 _____
5 _____

Extra Projects

1 _____
2 _____
3 _____

4 _____
5 _____

Week 8 From _____ _____ To _____ _____
            (Month)   (Day)   (Month)   (Day)

A. Home

1 _____
2 _____
3 _____
4 _____
5 _____

B. Health

1 _____
2 _____
3 _____
4 _____
5 _____

C. Personal and Fun

1 _____
2 _____
3 _____
4 _____
5 _____

D. Spiritual

1 _____
2 _____
3 _____
4 _____
5 _____

E. Finance

1 _____
2 _____
3 _____
4 _____
5 _____

F. Friends and Family

1 _____
2 _____
3 _____
4 _____
5 _____

G. Business

1 _____
2 _____
3 _____
4 _____
5 _____

H. Moving On

1 _____
2 _____
3 _____
4 _____
5 _____

I. "Free" Category

1 _____
2 _____
3 _____
4 _____
5 _____

Miracles this week

1 _____
2 _____
3 _____
4 _____
5 _____

Challenges this week

1 _____
2 _____
3 _____
4 _____
5 _____

Additional "to do"

1 _____
2 _____
3 _____
4 _____
5 _____

My successes this week

1 _____
2 _____
3 _____
4 _____
5 _____

Notes

1 _____
2 _____
3 _____
4 _____
5 _____

Extra Projects

1 _____
2 _____
3 _____

4 _____
5 _____

Week 9

From _____ _____
        (Month)   (Day)

To _____ _____
       (Month)   (Day)

A. Home

1 _____
2 _____
3 _____
4 _____
5 _____

B. Health

1 _____
2 _____
3 _____
4 _____
5 _____

C. Personal and Fun

1 _____
2 _____
3 _____
4 _____
5 _____

D. Spiritual

1 _____
2 _____
3 _____
4 _____
5 _____

E. Finance

1 _____
2 _____
3 _____
4 _____
5 _____

F. Friends and Family

1 _____
2 _____
3 _____
4 _____
5 _____

G. Business

1 _____
2 _____
3 _____
4 _____
5 _____

H. Moving On

1 _____
2 _____
3 _____
4 _____
5 _____

I. "Free" Category

1 _____
2 _____
3 _____
4 _____
5 _____

Miracles this week

1 _____
2 _____
3 _____
4 _____
5 _____

Challenges this week

1 _____
2 _____
3 _____
4 _____
5 _____

Additional "to do"

1 _____
2 _____
3 _____
4 _____
5 _____

My successes this week

1 _____
2 _____
3 _____
4 _____
5 _____

Notes

1 _____
2 _____
3 _____
4 _____
5 _____

Extra Projects

1 _____
2 _____
3 _____

4 _____
5 _____

Week 10

From

To

_____   _____   _____   _____
(Month)   (Day)   (Month)   (Day)

A. Home

1 _____
2 _____
3 _____
4 _____
5 _____

B. Health

1 _____
2 _____
3 _____
4 _____
5 _____

C. Personal and Fun

1 _____
2 _____
3 _____
4 _____
5 _____

D. Spiritual

1 _____
2 _____
3 _____
4 _____
5 _____

E. Finance

1 _____
2 _____
3 _____
4 _____
5 _____

F. Friends and Family

1 _____
2 _____
3 _____
4 _____
5 _____

G. Business

1 _____
2 _____
3 _____
4 _____
5 _____

H. Moving On

1 _____
2 _____
3 _____
4 _____
5 _____

I. "Free" Category

1 _____
2 _____
3 _____
4 _____
5 _____

Miracles this week

1 _____
2 _____
3 _____
4 _____
5 _____

Challenges this week

1 _____
2 _____
3 _____
4 _____
5 _____

Additional "to do"

1 _____
2 _____
3 _____
4 _____
5 _____

My successes this week

1 _____
2 _____
3 _____
4 _____
5 _____

Notes

1 _____
2 _____
3 _____
4 _____
5 _____

Extra Projects

1 _____
2 _____
3 _____

4 _____
5 _____

Week 11

From _____ _____
        (Month)   (Day)

To _____ _____
      (Month)   (Day)

A. Home

1 _____
2 _____
3 _____
4 _____
5 _____

B. Health

1 _____
2 _____
3 _____
4 _____
5 _____

C. Personal and Fun

1 _____
2 _____
3 _____
4 _____
5 _____

D. Spiritual

1 _____
2 _____
3 _____
4 _____
5 _____

E. Finance

1 _____
2 _____
3 _____
4 _____
5 _____

F. Friends and Family

1 _____
2 _____
3 _____
4 _____
5 _____

G. Business

1 _____
2 _____
3 _____
4 _____
5 _____

H. Moving On

1 _____
2 _____
3 _____
4 _____
5 _____

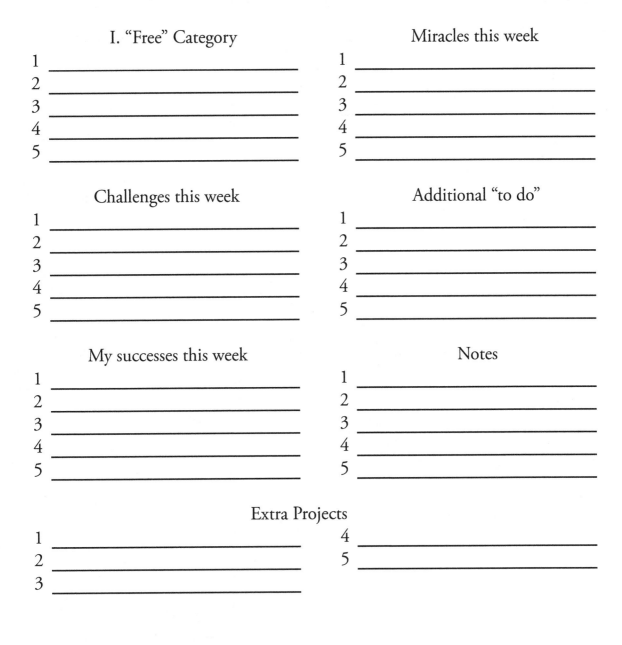

I. "Free" Category

1 _____
2 _____
3 _____
4 _____
5 _____

Miracles this week

1 _____
2 _____
3 _____
4 _____
5 _____

Challenges this week

1 _____
2 _____
3 _____
4 _____
5 _____

Additional "to do"

1 _____
2 _____
3 _____
4 _____
5 _____

My successes this week

1 _____
2 _____
3 _____
4 _____
5 _____

Notes

1 _____
2 _____
3 _____
4 _____
5 _____

Extra Projects

1 _____
2 _____
3 _____

4 _____
5 _____

Week 12

From _____ _____
        (Month)   (Day)

To _____ _____
        (Month)   (Day)

A. Home

1 _____
2 _____
3 _____
4 _____
5 _____

B. Health

1 _____
2 _____
3 _____
4 _____
5 _____

C. Personal and Fun

1 _____
2 _____
3 _____
4 _____
5 _____

D. Spiritual

1 _____
2 _____
3 _____
4 _____
5 _____

E. Finance

1 _____
2 _____
3 _____
4 _____
5 _____

F. Friends and Family

1 _____
2 _____
3 _____
4 _____
5 _____

G. Business

1 _____
2 _____
3 _____
4 _____
5 _____

H. Moving On

1 _____
2 _____
3 _____
4 _____
5 _____

I. "Free" Category

1 _____
2 _____
3 _____
4 _____
5 _____

Miracles this week

1 _____
2 _____
3 _____
4 _____
5 _____

Challenges this week

1 _____
2 _____
3 _____
4 _____
5 _____

Additional "to do"

1 _____
2 _____
3 _____
4 _____
5 _____

My successes this week

1 _____
2 _____
3 _____
4 _____
5 _____

Notes

1 _____
2 _____
3 _____
4 _____
5 _____

Extra Projects

1 _____
2 _____
3 _____

4 _____
5 _____

Week 13

From _____ _____   To _____ _____
         (Month)   (Day)   (Month)   (Day)

A. Home

1 _____
2 _____
3 _____
4 _____
5 _____

B. Health

1 _____
2 _____
3 _____
4 _____
5 _____

C. Personal and Fun

1 _____
2 _____
3 _____
4 _____
5 _____

D. Spiritual

1 _____
2 _____
3 _____
4 _____
5 _____

E. Finance

1 _____
2 _____
3 _____
4 _____
5 _____

F. Friends and Family

1 _____
2 _____
3 _____
4 _____
5 _____

G. Business

1 _____
2 _____
3 _____
4 _____
5 _____

H. Moving On

1 _____
2 _____
3 _____
4 _____
5 _____

I. "Free" Category

1 _____
2 _____
3 _____
4 _____
5 _____

Miracles this week

1 _____
2 _____
3 _____
4 _____
5 _____

Challenges this week

1 _____
2 _____
3 _____
4 _____
5 _____

Additional "to do"

1 _____
2 _____
3 _____
4 _____
5 _____

My successes this week

1 _____
2 _____
3 _____
4 _____
5 _____

Notes

1 _____
2 _____
3 _____
4 _____
5 _____

Extra Projects

1 _____
2 _____
3 _____

4 _____
5 _____

$\mathcal{S}$uccess is walking from failure with no loss of enthusiasm.

—Winston Churchill

$\mathcal{Y}$ou have not lived today until you have done something for someone who can never repay you.

—John Bunyan

This is great!

You have accomplished your first thirteen weeks of Perfect Planning 4 life!

1) Grab your partner and make a date to review your completed categories.

2) Have both of your "PP4Life" workbooks ready and marked (what has been completed, what are the struggles, and what needs to be looked at that you may be avoiding). All this is very revealing.

3) Open your workbook to the Master Categories Chart and write in the number of goals completed for your half-year wrap-up.

4) You may also want to pencil in the percent of what you have accomplished, and this will give you an idea if you are on schedule for the year or if you really have to start to focus on what you have not accomplished and why.

5) *Do not* be discouraged! Celebrate what you have accomplished and look at the items that are not accomplished:

   A. Is the timing off?

   B. Was it too aggressive?

   C. Will you be able to complete this goal later in the year?

   D. Be honest with yourself… This is how you grow.

Week 14
From _____ _____
       (Month)   (Day)

To _____ _____
       (Month)   (Day)

A. Home
1 _____
2 _____
3 _____
4 _____
5 _____

B. Health
1 _____
2 _____
3 _____
4 _____
5 _____

C. Personal and Fun
1 _____
2 _____
3 _____
4 _____
5 _____

D. Spiritual
1 _____
2 _____
3 _____
4 _____
5 _____

E. Finance
1 _____
2 _____
3 _____
4 _____
5 _____

F. Friends and Family
1 _____
2 _____
3 _____
4 _____
5 _____

G. Business
1 _____
2 _____
3 _____
4 _____
5 _____

H. Moving On
1 _____
2 _____
3 _____
4 _____
5 _____

I. "Free" Category

1 _____
2 _____
3 _____
4 _____
5 _____

Miracles this week

1 _____
2 _____
3 _____
4 _____
5 _____

Challenges this week

1 _____
2 _____
3 _____
4 _____
5 _____

Additional "to do"

1 _____
2 _____
3 _____
4 _____
5 _____

My successes this week

1 _____
2 _____
3 _____
4 _____
5 _____

Notes

1 _____
2 _____
3 _____
4 _____
5 _____

Extra Projects

1 _____
2 _____
3 _____

4 _____
5 _____

Week 15   From _____ _____   To _____ _____

(Month)   (Day)   (Month)   (Day)

A. Home

1 _____
2 _____
3 _____
4 _____
5 _____

B. Health

1 _____
2 _____
3 _____
4 _____
5 _____

C. Personal and Fun

1 _____
2 _____
3 _____
4 _____
5 _____

D. Spiritual

1 _____
2 _____
3 _____
4 _____
5 _____

E. Finance

1 _____
2 _____
3 _____
4 _____
5 _____

F. Friends and Family

1 _____
2 _____
3 _____
4 _____
5 _____

G. Business

1 _____
2 _____
3 _____
4 _____
5 _____

H. Moving On

1 _____
2 _____
3 _____
4 _____
5 _____

I. "Free" Category

1 _____
2 _____
3 _____
4 _____
5 _____

Miracles this week

1 _____
2 _____
3 _____
4 _____
5 _____

Challenges this week

1 _____
2 _____
3 _____
4 _____
5 _____

Additional "to do"

1 _____
2 _____
3 _____
4 _____
5 _____

My successes this week

1 _____
2 _____
3 _____
4 _____
5 _____

Notes

1 _____
2 _____
3 _____
4 _____
5 _____

Extra Projects

1 _____
2 _____
3 _____

4 _____
5 _____

Week 16

From _____ _____
(Month)   (Day)

To _____ _____
(Month)   (Day)

A. Home

1 _____
2 _____
3 _____
4 _____
5 _____

B. Health

1 _____
2 _____
3 _____
4 _____
5 _____

C. Personal and Fun

1 _____
2 _____
3 _____
4 _____
5 _____

D. Spiritual

1 _____
2 _____
3 _____
4 _____
5 _____

E. Finance

1 _____
2 _____
3 _____
4 _____
5 _____

F. Friends and Family

1 _____
2 _____
3 _____
4 _____
5 _____

G. Business

1 _____
2 _____
3 _____
4 _____
5 _____

H. Moving On

1 _____
2 _____
3 _____
4 _____
5 _____

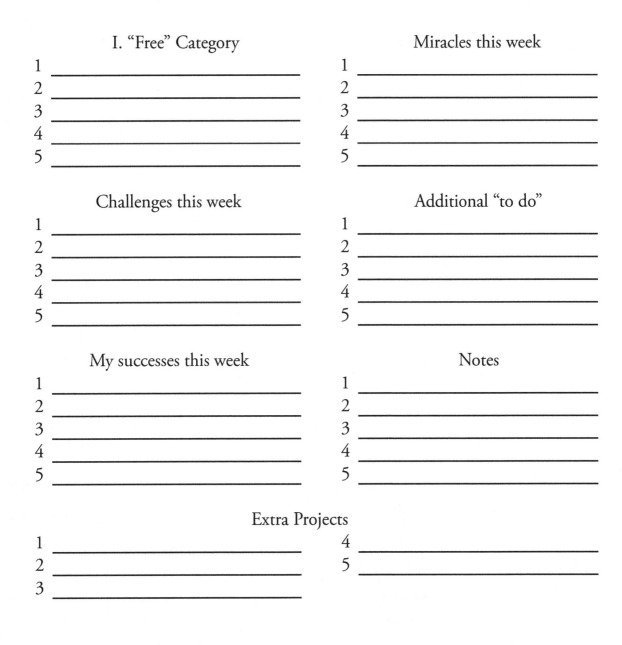

I. "Free" Category

1 _____
2 _____
3 _____
4 _____
5 _____

Miracles this week

1 _____
2 _____
3 _____
4 _____
5 _____

Challenges this week

1 _____
2 _____
3 _____
4 _____
5 _____

Additional "to do"

1 _____
2 _____
3 _____
4 _____
5 _____

My successes this week

1 _____
2 _____
3 _____
4 _____
5 _____

Notes

1 _____
2 _____
3 _____
4 _____
5 _____

Extra Projects

1 _____
2 _____
3 _____

4 _____
5 _____

Week 17 From _____ _____   To _____ _____
                    (Month)   (Day)   (Month)   (Day)

A. Home

1 _____
2 _____
3 _____
4 _____
5 _____

B. Health

1 _____
2 _____
3 _____
4 _____
5 _____

C. Personal and Fun

1 _____
2 _____
3 _____
4 _____
5 _____

D. Spiritual

1 _____
2 _____
3 _____
4 _____
5 _____

E. Finance

1 _____
2 _____
3 _____
4 _____
5 _____

F. Friends and Family

1 _____
2 _____
3 _____
4 _____
5 _____

G. Business

1 _____
2 _____
3 _____
4 _____
5 _____

H. Moving On

1 _____
2 _____
3 _____
4 _____
5 _____

I. "Free" Category

1 _____
2 _____
3 _____
4 _____
5 _____

Miracles this week

1 _____
2 _____
3 _____
4 _____
5 _____

Challenges this week

1 _____
2 _____
3 _____
4 _____
5 _____

Additional "to do"

1 _____
2 _____
3 _____
4 _____
5 _____

My successes this week

1 _____
2 _____
3 _____
4 _____
5 _____

Notes

1 _____
2 _____
3 _____
4 _____
5 _____

Extra Projects

1 _____
2 _____
3 _____

4 _____
5 _____

Week 18

From

To

(Month)   (Day)

(Month)   (Day)

A. Home

1 _____
2 _____
3 _____
4 _____
5 _____

E. Finance

1 _____
2 _____
3 _____
4 _____
5 _____

B. Health

1 _____
2 _____
3 _____
4 _____
5 _____

F. Friends and Family

1 _____
2 _____
3 _____
4 _____
5 _____

C. Personal and Fun

1 _____
2 _____
3 _____
4 _____
5 _____

G. Business

1 _____
2 _____
3 _____
4 _____
5 _____

D. Spiritual

1 _____
2 _____
3 _____
4 _____
5 _____

H. Moving On

1 _____
2 _____
3 _____
4 _____
5 _____

I. "Free" Category

1 _____
2 _____
3 _____
4 _____
5 _____

Miracles this week

1 _____
2 _____
3 _____
4 _____
5 _____

Challenges this week

1 _____
2 _____
3 _____
4 _____
5 _____

Additional "to do"

1 _____
2 _____
3 _____
4 _____
5 _____

My successes this week

1 _____
2 _____
3 _____
4 _____
5 _____

Notes

1 _____
2 _____
3 _____
4 _____
5 _____

Extra Projects

1 _____
2 _____
3 _____

4 _____
5 _____

Week 19

From _____ _____   To _____ _____
(Month)   (Day)   (Month)   (Day)

A. Home

1 _____
2 _____
3 _____
4 _____
5 _____

B. Health

1 _____
2 _____
3 _____
4 _____
5 _____

C. Personal and Fun

1 _____
2 _____
3 _____
4 _____
5 _____

D. Spiritual

1 _____
2 _____
3 _____
4 _____
5 _____

E. Finance

1 _____
2 _____
3 _____
4 _____
5 _____

F. Friends and Family

1 _____
2 _____
3 _____
4 _____
5 _____

G. Business

1 _____
2 _____
3 _____
4 _____
5 _____

H. Moving On

1 _____
2 _____
3 _____
4 _____
5 _____

I. "Free" Category

1 _____
2 _____
3 _____
4 _____
5 _____

Challenges this week

1 _____
2 _____
3 _____
4 _____
5 _____

My successes this week

1 _____
2 _____
3 _____
4 _____
5 _____

Miracles this week

1 _____
2 _____
3 _____
4 _____
5 _____

Additional "to do"

1 _____
2 _____
3 _____
4 _____
5 _____

Notes

1 _____
2 _____
3 _____
4 _____
5 _____

Extra Projects

1 _____
2 _____
3 _____

4 _____
5 _____

Week 20

From _____ _____
       (Month)   (Day)

To _____ _____
     (Month)   (Day)

A. Home

1 _____
2 _____
3 _____
4 _____
5 _____

B. Health

1 _____
2 _____
3 _____
4 _____
5 _____

C. Personal and Fun

1 _____
2 _____
3 _____
4 _____
5 _____

D. Spiritual

1 _____
2 _____
3 _____
4 _____
5 _____

E. Finance

1 _____
2 _____
3 _____
4 _____
5 _____

F. Friends and Family

1 _____
2 _____
3 _____
4 _____
5 _____

G. Business

1 _____
2 _____
3 _____
4 _____
5 _____

H. Moving On

1 _____
2 _____
3 _____
4 _____
5 _____

I. "Free" Category

1 _____
2 _____
3 _____
4 _____
5 _____

Miracles this week

1 _____
2 _____
3 _____
4 _____
5 _____

Challenges this week

1 _____
2 _____
3 _____
4 _____
5 _____

Additional "to do"

1 _____
2 _____
3 _____
4 _____
5 _____

My successes this week

1 _____
2 _____
3 _____
4 _____
5 _____

Notes

1 _____
2 _____
3 _____
4 _____
5 _____

Extra Projects

1 _____
2 _____
3 _____

4 _____
5 _____

Week 21 From _____ _____   To _____ _____
                    (Month)   (Day)   (Month)   (Day)

A. Home

1 _____
2 _____
3 _____
4 _____
5 _____

B. Health

1 _____
2 _____
3 _____
4 _____
5 _____

C. Personal and Fun

1 _____
2 _____
3 _____
4 _____
5 _____

D. Spiritual

1 _____
2 _____
3 _____
4 _____
5 _____

E. Finance

1 _____
2 _____
3 _____
4 _____
5 _____

F. Friends and Family

1 _____
2 _____
3 _____
4 _____
5 _____

G. Business

1 _____
2 _____
3 _____
4 _____
5 _____

H. Moving On

1 _____
2 _____
3 _____
4 _____
5 _____

I. "Free" Category

1 _____
2 _____
3 _____
4 _____
5 _____

Miracles this week

1 _____
2 _____
3 _____
4 _____
5 _____

Challenges this week

1 _____
2 _____
3 _____
4 _____
5 _____

Additional "to do"

1 _____
2 _____
3 _____
4 _____
5 _____

My successes this week

1 _____
2 _____
3 _____
4 _____
5 _____

Notes

1 _____
2 _____
3 _____
4 _____
5 _____

Extra Projects

1 _____
2 _____
3 _____

4 _____
5 _____

Week 22

From _____ _____
(Month)   (Day)

To _____ _____
(Month)   (Day)

A. Home

1 _____
2 _____
3 _____
4 _____
5 _____

B. Health

1 _____
2 _____
3 _____
4 _____
5 _____

C. Personal and Fun

1 _____
2 _____
3 _____
4 _____
5 _____

D. Spiritual

1 _____
2 _____
3 _____
4 _____
5 _____

E. Finance

1 _____
2 _____
3 _____
4 _____
5 _____

F. Friends and Family

1 _____
2 _____
3 _____
4 _____
5 _____

G. Business

1 _____
2 _____
3 _____
4 _____
5 _____

H. Moving On

1 _____
2 _____
3 _____
4 _____
5 _____

I. "Free" Category

1 _____
2 _____
3 _____
4 _____
5 _____

Miracles this week

1 _____
2 _____
3 _____
4 _____
5 _____

Challenges this week

1 _____
2 _____
3 _____
4 _____
5 _____

Additional "to do"

1 _____
2 _____
3 _____
4 _____
5 _____

My successes this week

1 _____
2 _____
3 _____
4 _____
5 _____

Notes

1 _____
2 _____
3 _____
4 _____
5 _____

Extra Projects

1 _____
2 _____
3 _____

4 _____
5 _____

Week 23

From
_____ _____
(Month)   (Day)

To
_____ _____
(Month)   (Day)

A. Home

1 _____
2 _____
3 _____
4 _____
5 _____

B. Health

1 _____
2 _____
3 _____
4 _____
5 _____

C. Personal and Fun

1 _____
2 _____
3 _____
4 _____
5 _____

D. Spiritual

1 _____
2 _____
3 _____
4 _____
5 _____

E. Finance

1 _____
2 _____
3 _____
4 _____
5 _____

F. Friends and Family

1 _____
2 _____
3 _____
4 _____
5 _____

G. Business

1 _____
2 _____
3 _____
4 _____
5 _____

H. Moving On

1 _____
2 _____
3 _____
4 _____
5 _____

I. "Free" Category

1 _____
2 _____
3 _____
4 _____
5 _____

Challenges this week

1 _____
2 _____
3 _____
4 _____
5 _____

My successes this week

1 _____
2 _____
3 _____
4 _____
5 _____

Miracles this week

1 _____
2 _____
3 _____
4 _____
5 _____

Additional "to do"

1 _____
2 _____
3 _____
4 _____
5 _____

Notes

1 _____
2 _____
3 _____
4 _____
5 _____

Extra Projects

1 _____
2 _____
3 _____

4 _____
5 _____

Week 24

From _____ _____
      (Month)   (Day)

To _____ _____
      (Month)   (Day)

A. Home

1 _____
2 _____
3 _____
4 _____
5 _____

B. Health

1 _____
2 _____
3 _____
4 _____
5 _____

C. Personal and Fun

1 _____
2 _____
3 _____
4 _____
5 _____

D. Spiritual

1 _____
2 _____
3 _____
4 _____
5 _____

E. Finance

1 _____
2 _____
3 _____
4 _____
5 _____

F. Friends and Family

1 _____
2 _____
3 _____
4 _____
5 _____

G. Business

1 _____
2 _____
3 _____
4 _____
5 _____

H. Moving On

1 _____
2 _____
3 _____
4 _____
5 _____

I. "Free" Category

1 _____
2 _____
3 _____
4 _____
5 _____

Miracles this week

1 _____
2 _____
3 _____
4 _____
5 _____

Challenges this week

1 _____
2 _____
3 _____
4 _____
5 _____

Additional "to do"

1 _____
2 _____
3 _____
4 _____
5 _____

My successes this week

1 _____
2 _____
3 _____
4 _____
5 _____

Notes

1 _____
2 _____
3 _____
4 _____
5 _____

Extra Projects

1 _____
2 _____
3 _____

4 _____
5 _____

Week 25

From
_____ _____
(Month)   (Day)

To
_____ _____
(Month)   (Day)

A. Home
1 _____
2 _____
3 _____
4 _____
5 _____

B. Health
1 _____
2 _____
3 _____
4 _____
5 _____

C. Personal and Fun
1 _____
2 _____
3 _____
4 _____
5 _____

D. Spiritual
1 _____
2 _____
3 _____
4 _____
5 _____

E. Finance
1 _____
2 _____
3 _____
4 _____
5 _____

F. Friends and Family
1 _____
2 _____
3 _____
4 _____
5 _____

G. Business
1 _____
2 _____
3 _____
4 _____
5 _____

H. Moving On
1 _____
2 _____
3 _____
4 _____
5 _____

I. "Free" Category

1 _____
2 _____
3 _____
4 _____
5 _____

Challenges this week

1 _____
2 _____
3 _____
4 _____
5 _____

My successes this week

1 _____
2 _____
3 _____
4 _____
5 _____

Miracles this week

1 _____
2 _____
3 _____
4 _____
5 _____

Additional "to do"

1 _____
2 _____
3 _____
4 _____
5 _____

Notes

1 _____
2 _____
3 _____
4 _____
5 _____

Extra Projects

1 _____
2 _____
3 _____

4 _____
5 _____

Week 26

From

To

(Month)　　　(Day)　　　　　(Month)　　　(Day)

A. Home

1 _____
2 _____
3 _____
4 _____
5 _____

E. Finance

1 _____
2 _____
3 _____
4 _____
5 _____

B. Health

1 _____
2 _____
3 _____
4 _____
5 _____

F. Friends and Family

1 _____
2 _____
3 _____
4 _____
5 _____

C. Personal and Fun

1 _____
2 _____
3 _____
4 _____
5 _____

G. Business

1 _____
2 _____
3 _____
4 _____
5 _____

D. Spiritual

1 _____
2 _____
3 _____
4 _____
5 _____

H. Moving On

1 _____
2 _____
3 _____
4 _____
5 _____

I. "Free" Category

1 _____
2 _____
3 _____
4 _____
5 _____

Miracles this week

1 _____
2 _____
3 _____
4 _____
5 _____

Challenges this week

1 _____
2 _____
3 _____
4 _____
5 _____

Additional "to do"

1 _____
2 _____
3 _____
4 _____
5 _____

My successes this week

1 _____
2 _____
3 _____
4 _____
5 _____

Notes

1 _____
2 _____
3 _____
4 _____
5 _____

Extra Projects

1 _____
2 _____
3 _____

4 _____
5 _____

You will never do anything in this world without courage. It is the greatest quality of the mind next to honor.

—Aristotle

Half-Year Review (26 Weeks)

This is great!

     You have accomplished your first twenty-six weeks of Perfect Planning 4 life!

1) Grab your partner and make a date to review your completed categories.

2) Have both of your "PP4Life" workbooks ready and marked (what has been completed, what are the struggles, and what needs to be looked at that you may be avoiding). All this is very revealing.

3) Open your workbook to the Master Categories Chart and write in the number of goals completed for your half-year wrap-up.

4) You may also want to pencil in the percent of what you have accomplished, and this will give you an idea if you are on schedule for the year or if you really have to start to focus on what you have not accomplished and why.

5) *Do not* be discouraged! Celebrate what you have accomplished and look at the items that are not accomplished and why.

    A. Is the timing off?

    B. Was it too aggressive?

    C. Will you be able to complete this goal at a later time in the year?

    D. Be honest with yourself… This is how you grow.

Do you love this!

Week 27
From _____ _____
(Month) (Day)

To _____ _____
(Month) (Day)

A. Home

1 _____
2 _____
3 _____
4 _____
5 _____

B. Health

1 _____
2 _____
3 _____
4 _____
5 _____

C. Personal and Fun

1 _____
2 _____
3 _____
4 _____
5 _____

D. Spiritual

1 _____
2 _____
3 _____
4 _____
5 _____

E. Finance

1 _____
2 _____
3 _____
4 _____
5 _____

F. Friends and Family

1 _____
2 _____
3 _____
4 _____
5 _____

G. Business

1 _____
2 _____
3 _____
4 _____
5 _____

H. Moving On

1 _____
2 _____
3 _____
4 _____
5 _____

I. "Free" Category

1 _____
2 _____
3 _____
4 _____
5 _____

Miracles this week

1 _____
2 _____
3 _____
4 _____
5 _____

Challenges this week

1 _____
2 _____
3 _____
4 _____
5 _____

Additional "to do"

1 _____
2 _____
3 _____
4 _____
5 _____

My successes this week

1 _____
2 _____
3 _____
4 _____
5 _____

Notes

1 _____
2 _____
3 _____
4 _____
5 _____

Extra Projects

1 _____
2 _____
3 _____

4 _____
5 _____

Week 28 From _____ _____ To _____ _____
(Month) (Day) (Month) (Day)

A. Home

1 _____
2 _____
3 _____
4 _____
5 _____

B. Health

1 _____
2 _____
3 _____
4 _____
5 _____

C. Personal and Fun

1 _____
2 _____
3 _____
4 _____
5 _____

D. Spiritual

1 _____
2 _____
3 _____
4 _____
5 _____

E. Finance

1 _____
2 _____
3 _____
4 _____
5 _____

F. Friends and Family

1 _____
2 _____
3 _____
4 _____
5 _____

G. Business

1 _____
2 _____
3 _____
4 _____
5 _____

H. Moving On

1 _____
2 _____
3 _____
4 _____
5 _____

I. "Free" Category

1 _____
2 _____
3 _____
4 _____
5 _____

Miracles this week

1 _____
2 _____
3 _____
4 _____
5 _____

Challenges this week

1 _____
2 _____
3 _____
4 _____
5 _____

Additional "to do"

1 _____
2 _____
3 _____
4 _____
5 _____

My successes this week

1 _____
2 _____
3 _____
4 _____
5 _____

Notes

1 _____
2 _____
3 _____
4 _____
5 _____

Extra Projects

1 _____
2 _____
3 _____

4 _____
5 _____

Week 29

From _____ _____
       (Month)   (Day)

To _____ _____
     (Month)   (Day)

A. Home

1 _____
2 _____
3 _____
4 _____
5 _____

B. Health

1 _____
2 _____
3 _____
4 _____
5 _____

C. Personal and Fun

1 _____
2 _____
3 _____
4 _____
5 _____

D. Spiritual

1 _____
2 _____
3 _____
4 _____
5 _____

E. Finance

1 _____
2 _____
3 _____
4 _____
5 _____

F. Friends and Family

1 _____
2 _____
3 _____
4 _____
5 _____

G. Business

1 _____
2 _____
3 _____
4 _____
5 _____

H. Moving On

1 _____
2 _____
3 _____
4 _____
5 _____

I. "Free" Category

1 _____
2 _____
3 _____
4 _____
5 _____

Miracles this week

1 _____
2 _____
3 _____
4 _____
5 _____

Challenges this week

1 _____
2 _____
3 _____
4 _____
5 _____

Additional "to do"

1 _____
2 _____
3 _____
4 _____
5 _____

My successes this week

1 _____
2 _____
3 _____
4 _____
5 _____

Notes

1 _____
2 _____
3 _____
4 _____
5 _____

Extra Projects

1 _____
2 _____
3 _____

4 _____
5 _____

Week 30

From
_____ _____
(Month)   (Day)

To
_____ _____
(Month)   (Day)

A. Home

1 _____
2 _____
3 _____
4 _____
5 _____

B. Health

1 _____
2 _____
3 _____
4 _____
5 _____

C. Personal and Fun

1 _____
2 _____
3 _____
4 _____
5 _____

D. Spiritual

1 _____
2 _____
3 _____
4 _____
5 _____

E. Finance

1 _____
2 _____
3 _____
4 _____
5 _____

F. Friends and Family

1 _____
2 _____
3 _____
4 _____
5 _____

G. Business

1 _____
2 _____
3 _____
4 _____
5 _____

H. Moving On

1 _____
2 _____
3 _____
4 _____
5 _____

I. "Free" Category

1 _____
2 _____
3 _____
4 _____
5 _____

Miracles this week

1 _____
2 _____
3 _____
4 _____
5 _____

Challenges this week

1 _____
2 _____
3 _____
4 _____
5 _____

Additional "to do"

1 _____
2 _____
3 _____
4 _____
5 _____

My successes this week

1 _____
2 _____
3 _____
4 _____
5 _____

Notes

1 _____
2 _____
3 _____
4 _____
5 _____

Extra Projects

1 _____
2 _____
3 _____

4 _____
5 _____

Week 31

From _____ _____   To _____ _____
        (Month)   (Day)   (Month)   (Day)

A. Home

1 _____
2 _____
3 _____
4 _____
5 _____

B. Health

1 _____
2 _____
3 _____
4 _____
5 _____

C. Personal and Fun

1 _____
2 _____
3 _____
4 _____
5 _____

D. Spiritual

1 _____
2 _____
3 _____
4 _____
5 _____

E. Finance

1 _____
2 _____
3 _____
4 _____
5 _____

F. Friends and Family

1 _____
2 _____
3 _____
4 _____
5 _____

G. Business

1 _____
2 _____
3 _____
4 _____
5 _____

H. Moving On

1 _____
2 _____
3 _____
4 _____
5 _____

I. "Free" Category

1 _____
2 _____
3 _____
4 _____
5 _____

Miracles this week

1 _____
2 _____
3 _____
4 _____
5 _____

Challenges this week

1 _____
2 _____
3 _____
4 _____
5 _____

Additional "to do"

1 _____
2 _____
3 _____
4 _____
5 _____

My successes this week

1 _____
2 _____
3 _____
4 _____
5 _____

Notes

1 _____
2 _____
3 _____
4 _____
5 _____

Extra Projects

1 _____
2 _____
3 _____

4 _____
5 _____

Week 32   From _____ _____   To _____ _____
                    (Month)   (Day)   (Month)   (Day)

A. Home

1 _____
2 _____
3 _____
4 _____
5 _____

B. Health

1 _____
2 _____
3 _____
4 _____
5 _____

C. Personal and Fun

1 _____
2 _____
3 _____
4 _____
5 _____

D. Spiritual

1 _____
2 _____
3 _____
4 _____
5 _____

E. Finance

1 _____
2 _____
3 _____
4 _____
5 _____

F. Friends and Family

1 _____
2 _____
3 _____
4 _____
5 _____

G. Business

1 _____
2 _____
3 _____
4 _____
5 _____

H. Moving On

1 _____
2 _____
3 _____
4 _____
5 _____

I. "Free" Category

1 _____
2 _____
3 _____
4 _____
5 _____

Miracles this week

1 _____
2 _____
3 _____
4 _____
5 _____

Challenges this week

1 _____
2 _____
3 _____
4 _____
5 _____

Additional "to do"

1 _____
2 _____
3 _____
4 _____
5 _____

My successes this week

1 _____
2 _____
3 _____
4 _____
5 _____

Notes

1 _____
2 _____
3 _____
4 _____
5 _____

Extra Projects

1 _____
2 _____
3 _____

4 _____
5 _____

Week 33

From _____ _____
         (Month)   (Day)

To _____ _____
        (Month)   (Day)

A. Home

1 _____
2 _____
3 _____
4 _____
5 _____

B. Health

1 _____
2 _____
3 _____
4 _____
5 _____

C. Personal and Fun

1 _____
2 _____
3 _____
4 _____
5 _____

D. Spiritual

1 _____
2 _____
3 _____
4 _____
5 _____

E. Finance

1 _____
2 _____
3 _____
4 _____
5 _____

F. Friends and Family

1 _____
2 _____
3 _____
4 _____
5 _____

G. Business

1 _____
2 _____
3 _____
4 _____
5 _____

H. Moving On

1 _____
2 _____
3 _____
4 _____
5 _____

I. "Free" Category

1 _____
2 _____
3 _____
4 _____
5 _____

Challenges this week

1 _____
2 _____
3 _____
4 _____
5 _____

My successes this week

1 _____
2 _____
3 _____
4 _____
5 _____

Miracles this week

1 _____
2 _____
3 _____
4 _____
5 _____

Additional "to do"

1 _____
2 _____
3 _____
4 _____
5 _____

Notes

1 _____
2 _____
3 _____
4 _____
5 _____

Extra Projects

1 _____
2 _____
3 _____

4 _____
5 _____

Week 34　From _____ _____　To _____ _____
　　　　　　　　(Month)　　　　(Day)　　　　　　(Month)　　　　(Day)

A. Home

1 _____
2 _____
3 _____
4 _____
5 _____

B. Health

1 _____
2 _____
3 _____
4 _____
5 _____

C. Personal and Fun

1 _____
2 _____
3 _____
4 _____
5 _____

D. Spiritual

1 _____
2 _____
3 _____
4 _____
5 _____

E. Finance

1 _____
2 _____
3 _____
4 _____
5 _____

F. Friends and Family

1 _____
2 _____
3 _____
4 _____
5 _____

G. Business

1 _____
2 _____
3 _____
4 _____
5 _____

H. Moving On

1 _____
2 _____
3 _____
4 _____
5 _____

I. "Free" Category

1 _____
2 _____
3 _____
4 _____
5 _____

Miracles this week

1 _____
2 _____
3 _____
4 _____
5 _____

Challenges this week

1 _____
2 _____
3 _____
4 _____
5 _____

Additional "to do"

1 _____
2 _____
3 _____
4 _____
5 _____

My successes this week

1 _____
2 _____
3 _____
4 _____
5 _____

Notes

1 _____
2 _____
3 _____
4 _____
5 _____

Extra Projects

1 _____
2 _____
3 _____

4 _____
5 _____

Week 35

From
_____ _____
(Month)   (Day)

To
_____ _____
(Month)   (Day)

A. Home

1 _____
2 _____
3 _____
4 _____
5 _____

B. Health

1 _____
2 _____
3 _____
4 _____
5 _____

C. Personal and Fun

1 _____
2 _____
3 _____
4 _____
5 _____

D. Spiritual

1 _____
2 _____
3 _____
4 _____
5 _____

E. Finance

1 _____
2 _____
3 _____
4 _____
5 _____

F. Friends and Family

1 _____
2 _____
3 _____
4 _____
5 _____

G. Business

1 _____
2 _____
3 _____
4 _____
5 _____

H. Moving On

1 _____
2 _____
3 _____
4 _____
5 _____

I. "Free" Category

1 _____
2 _____
3 _____
4 _____
5 _____

Miracles this week

1 _____
2 _____
3 _____
4 _____
5 _____

Challenges this week

1 _____
2 _____
3 _____
4 _____
5 _____

Additional "to do"

1 _____
2 _____
3 _____
4 _____
5 _____

My successes this week

1 _____
2 _____
3 _____
4 _____
5 _____

Notes

1 _____
2 _____
3 _____
4 _____
5 _____

Extra Projects

1 _____
2 _____
3 _____

4 _____
5 _____

Week 36 From _____ _____   To _____ _____
                    (Month)   (Day)   (Month)   (Day)

A. Home
1 _____
2 _____
3 _____
4 _____
5 _____

B. Health
1 _____
2 _____
3 _____
4 _____
5 _____

C. Personal and Fun
1 _____
2 _____
3 _____
4 _____
5 _____

D. Spiritual
1 _____
2 _____
3 _____
4 _____
5 _____

E. Finance
1 _____
2 _____
3 _____
4 _____
5 _____

F. Friends and Family
1 _____
2 _____
3 _____
4 _____
5 _____

G. Business
1 _____
2 _____
3 _____
4 _____
5 _____

H. Moving On
1 _____
2 _____
3 _____
4 _____
5 _____

I. "Free" Category

1 _____
2 _____
3 _____
4 _____
5 _____

Miracles this week

1 _____
2 _____
3 _____
4 _____
5 _____

Challenges this week

1 _____
2 _____
3 _____
4 _____
5 _____

Additional "to do"

1 _____
2 _____
3 _____
4 _____
5 _____

My successes this week

1 _____
2 _____
3 _____
4 _____
5 _____

Notes

1 _____
2 _____
3 _____
4 _____
5 _____

Extra Projects

1 _____
2 _____
3 _____

4 _____
5 _____

Week 37

From _____ _____
       (Month)   (Day)

To _____ _____
     (Month)   (Day)

A. Home

1 _____
2 _____
3 _____
4 _____
5 _____

B. Health

1 _____
2 _____
3 _____
4 _____
5 _____

C. Personal and Fun

1 _____
2 _____
3 _____
4 _____
5 _____

D. Spiritual

1 _____
2 _____
3 _____
4 _____
5 _____

E. Finance

1 _____
2 _____
3 _____
4 _____
5 _____

F. Friends and Family

1 _____
2 _____
3 _____
4 _____
5 _____

G. Business

1 _____
2 _____
3 _____
4 _____
5 _____

H. Moving On

1 _____
2 _____
3 _____
4 _____
5 _____

I. "Free" Category

1 _____
2 _____
3 _____
4 _____
5 _____

Miracles this week

1 _____
2 _____
3 _____
4 _____
5 _____

Challenges this week

1 _____
2 _____
3 _____
4 _____
5 _____

Additional "to do"

1 _____
2 _____
3 _____
4 _____
5 _____

My successes this week

1 _____
2 _____
3 _____
4 _____
5 _____

Notes

1 _____
2 _____
3 _____
4 _____
5 _____

Extra Projects

1 _____
2 _____
3 _____

4 _____
5 _____

Week 38

From _____ _____
(Month)   (Day)

To _____ _____
(Month)   (Day)

A. Home

1 _____
2 _____
3 _____
4 _____
5 _____

B. Health

1 _____
2 _____
3 _____
4 _____
5 _____

C. Personal and Fun

1 _____
2 _____
3 _____
4 _____
5 _____

D. Spiritual

1 _____
2 _____
3 _____
4 _____
5 _____

E. Finance

1 _____
2 _____
3 _____
4 _____
5 _____

F. Friends and Family

1 _____
2 _____
3 _____
4 _____
5 _____

G. Business

1 _____
2 _____
3 _____
4 _____
5 _____

H. Moving On

1 _____
2 _____
3 _____
4 _____
5 _____

I. "Free" Category

1 _____
2 _____
3 _____
4 _____
5 _____

Miracles this week

1 _____
2 _____
3 _____
4 _____
5 _____

Challenges this week

1 _____
2 _____
3 _____
4 _____
5 _____

Additional "to do"

1 _____
2 _____
3 _____
4 _____
5 _____

My successes this week

1 _____
2 _____
3 _____
4 _____
5 _____

Notes

1 _____
2 _____
3 _____
4 _____
5 _____

Extra Projects

1 _____
2 _____
3 _____

4 _____
5 _____

Week 39

From

_____ _____
(Month)   (Day)

To

_____ _____
(Month)   (Day)

A. Home

1 _____
2 _____
3 _____
4 _____
5 _____

B. Health

1 _____
2 _____
3 _____
4 _____
5 _____

C. Personal and Fun

1 _____
2 _____
3 _____
4 _____
5 _____

D. Spiritual

1 _____
2 _____
3 _____
4 _____
5 _____

E. Finance

1 _____
2 _____
3 _____
4 _____
5 _____

F. Friends and Family

1 _____
2 _____
3 _____
4 _____
5 _____

G. Business

1 _____
2 _____
3 _____
4 _____
5 _____

H. Moving On

1 _____
2 _____
3 _____
4 _____
5 _____

I. "Free" Category

1 _____
2 _____
3 _____
4 _____
5 _____

Miracles this week

1 _____
2 _____
3 _____
4 _____
5 _____

Challenges this week

1 _____
2 _____
3 _____
4 _____
5 _____

Additional "to do"

1 _____
2 _____
3 _____
4 _____
5 _____

My successes this week

1 _____
2 _____
3 _____
4 _____
5 _____

Notes

1 _____
2 _____
3 _____
4 _____
5 _____

Extra Projects

1 _____
2 _____
3 _____

4 _____
5 _____

*L*ife is Choice Driven, Choose Wisely
and live with Great Intension.

—Tina Russek

*E*very adversity, every failure, every heartache carries
with it the seed of an equal or greater benefit.

—Napoleon Hill

*G*reat works are performed not by strength but by perseverance.

—Samuel Johnson

This is great!

    You have accomplished your first thirty-nine weeks of perfect planning.

1) Grab your partner and make a date to review your completed categories.

2) Have both of your "PP4Life" workbooks ready and marked (what has been completed, what are the struggles, and what needs to be looked at that you may be avoiding). All this is very revealing.

3) Open your workbook to the Master Categories Chart and write in the number of goals completed for your three-quarter-year wrap-up.

4) You may also want to pencil in the percent of what you have accomplished, and this will give you an idea of if you are on schedule for the year or if you really have to start to focus on what you have not accomplished and why.

5) *Do not* be discouraged! Celebrate what you have accomplished and look at the items that are not accomplished:

    A. Is the timing off?

    B. Was it too aggressive?

    C. Will you be able to complete this goal later in the year?

    D. Be honest with yourself… This is how you grow.

Week 40 From _____ _____ To _____ _____
(Month) (Day) (Month) (Day)

A. Home

1 _____
2 _____
3 _____
4 _____
5 _____

B. Health

1 _____
2 _____
3 _____
4 _____
5 _____

C. Personal and Fun

1 _____
2 _____
3 _____
4 _____
5 _____

D. Spiritual

1 _____
2 _____
3 _____
4 _____
5 _____

E. Finance

1 _____
2 _____
3 _____
4 _____
5 _____

F. Friends and Family

1 _____
2 _____
3 _____
4 _____
5 _____

G. Business

1 _____
2 _____
3 _____
4 _____
5 _____

H. Moving On

1 _____
2 _____
3 _____
4 _____
5 _____

I. "Free" Category

1 _____
2 _____
3 _____
4 _____
5 _____

Miracles this week

1 _____
2 _____
3 _____
4 _____
5 _____

Challenges this week

1 _____
2 _____
3 _____
4 _____
5 _____

Additional "to do"

1 _____
2 _____
3 _____
4 _____
5 _____

My successes this week

1 _____
2 _____
3 _____
4 _____
5 _____

Notes

1 _____
2 _____
3 _____
4 _____
5 _____

Extra Projects

1 _____
2 _____
3 _____
4 _____
5 _____

Week 41

From
_____ _____
(Month)   (Day)

To
_____ _____
(Month)   (Day)

A. Home

1 _____
2 _____
3 _____
4 _____
5 _____

B. Health

1 _____
2 _____
3 _____
4 _____
5 _____

C. Personal and Fun

1 _____
2 _____
3 _____
4 _____
5 _____

D. Spiritual

1 _____
2 _____
3 _____
4 _____
5 _____

E. Finance

1 _____
2 _____
3 _____
4 _____
5 _____

F. Friends and Family

1 _____
2 _____
3 _____
4 _____
5 _____

G. Business

1 _____
2 _____
3 _____
4 _____
5 _____

H. Moving On

1 _____
2 _____
3 _____
4 _____
5 _____

I. "Free" Category

1 _____
2 _____
3 _____
4 _____
5 _____

Miracles this week

1 _____
2 _____
3 _____
4 _____
5 _____

Challenges this week

1 _____
2 _____
3 _____
4 _____
5 _____

Additional "to do"

1 _____
2 _____
3 _____
4 _____
5 _____

My successes this week

1 _____
2 _____
3 _____
4 _____
5 _____

Notes

1 _____
2 _____
3 _____
4 _____
5 _____

Extra Projects

1 _____
2 _____
3 _____

4 _____
5 _____

Week 42 From _____ _____   To _____ _____
                    (Month)   (Day)   (Month)   (Day)

A. Home

1 _____
2 _____
3 _____
4 _____
5 _____

B. Health

1 _____
2 _____
3 _____
4 _____
5 _____

C. Personal and Fun

1 _____
2 _____
3 _____
4 _____
5 _____

D. Spiritual

1 _____
2 _____
3 _____
4 _____
5 _____

E. Finance

1 _____
2 _____
3 _____
4 _____
5 _____

F. Friends and Family

1 _____
2 _____
3 _____
4 _____
5 _____

G. Business

1 _____
2 _____
3 _____
4 _____
5 _____

H. Moving On

1 _____
2 _____
3 _____
4 _____
5 _____

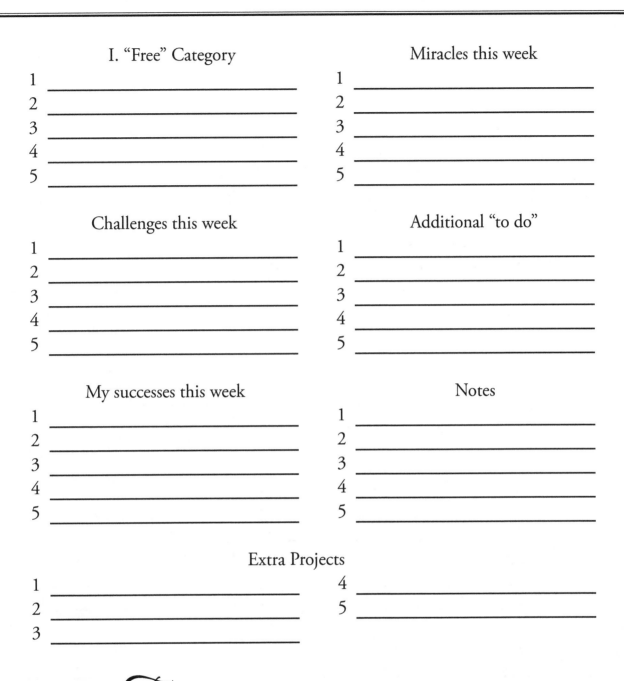

I. "Free" Category

1 _____
2 _____
3 _____
4 _____
5 _____

Miracles this week

1 _____
2 _____
3 _____
4 _____
5 _____

Challenges this week

1 _____
2 _____
3 _____
4 _____
5 _____

Additional "to do"

1 _____
2 _____
3 _____
4 _____
5 _____

My successes this week

1 _____
2 _____
3 _____
4 _____
5 _____

Notes

1 _____
2 _____
3 _____
4 _____
5 _____

Extra Projects

1 _____
2 _____
3 _____

4 _____
5 _____

*T*hink twice before you speak because your
words and influence will plant the seed of either
success or failure in the mind of another.

—Napoleon Hill

Be aware of the power you have every day.

Week 43 From _____ _____ To _____ _____
                    (Month)   (Day)   (Month)   (Day)

A. Home

1 _____
2 _____
3 _____
4 _____
5 _____

B. Health

1 _____
2 _____
3 _____
4 _____
5 _____

C. Personal and Fun

1 _____
2 _____
3 _____
4 _____
5 _____

D. Spiritual

1 _____
2 _____
3 _____
4 _____
5 _____

E. Finance

1 _____
2 _____
3 _____
4 _____
5 _____

F. Friends and Family

1 _____
2 _____
3 _____
4 _____
5 _____

G. Business

1 _____
2 _____
3 _____
4 _____
5 _____

H. Moving On

1 _____
2 _____
3 _____
4 _____
5 _____

I. "Free" Category

1 _____
2 _____
3 _____
4 _____
5 _____

Miracles this week

1 _____
2 _____
3 _____
4 _____
5 _____

Challenges this week

1 _____
2 _____
3 _____
4 _____
5 _____

Additional "to do"

1 _____
2 _____
3 _____
4 _____
5 _____

My successes this week

1 _____
2 _____
3 _____
4 _____
5 _____

Notes

1 _____
2 _____
3 _____
4 _____
5 _____

Extra Projects

1 _____
2 _____
3 _____

4 _____
5 _____

Week 44   From _____ _____   To _____ _____
                    (Month)   (Day)   (Month)   (Day)

A. Home

1 _____
2 _____
3 _____
4 _____
5 _____

B. Health

1 _____
2 _____
3 _____
4 _____
5 _____

C. Personal and Fun

1 _____
2 _____
3 _____
4 _____
5 _____

D. Spiritual

1 _____
2 _____
3 _____
4 _____
5 _____

E. Finance

1 _____
2 _____
3 _____
4 _____
5 _____

F. Friends and Family

1 _____
2 _____
3 _____
4 _____
5 _____

G. Business

1 _____
2 _____
3 _____
4 _____
5 _____

H. Moving On

1 _____
2 _____
3 _____
4 _____
5 _____

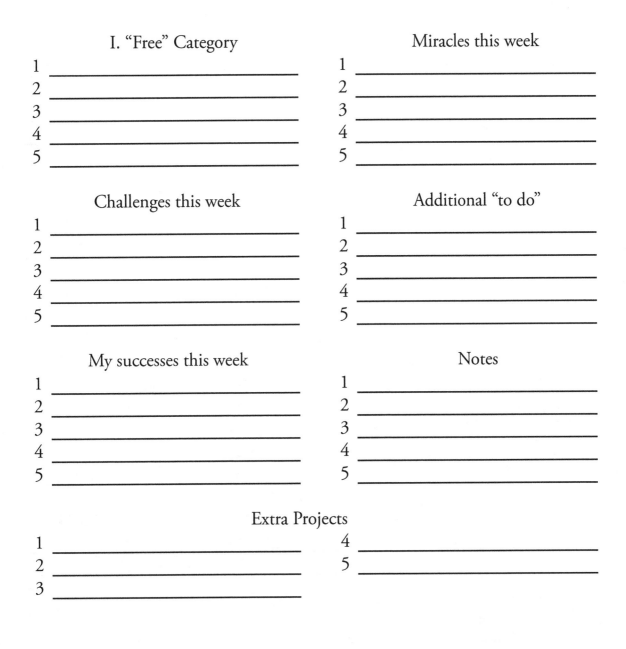

I. "Free" Category

1 _____
2 _____
3 _____
4 _____
5 _____

Miracles this week

1 _____
2 _____
3 _____
4 _____
5 _____

Challenges this week

1 _____
2 _____
3 _____
4 _____
5 _____

Additional "to do"

1 _____
2 _____
3 _____
4 _____
5 _____

My successes this week

1 _____
2 _____
3 _____
4 _____
5 _____

Notes

1 _____
2 _____
3 _____
4 _____
5 _____

Extra Projects

1 _____
2 _____
3 _____

4 _____
5 _____

Week 45

From

To

(Month)   (Day)

(Month)   (Day)

A. Home

1 _____
2 _____
3 _____
4 _____
5 _____

E. Finance

1 _____
2 _____
3 _____
4 _____
5 _____

B. Health

1 _____
2 _____
3 _____
4 _____
5 _____

F. Friends and Family

1 _____
2 _____
3 _____
4 _____
5 _____

C. Personal and Fun

1 _____
2 _____
3 _____
4 _____
5 _____

G. Business

1 _____
2 _____
3 _____
4 _____
5 _____

D. Spiritual

1 _____
2 _____
3 _____
4 _____
5 _____

H. Moving On

1 _____
2 _____
3 _____
4 _____
5 _____

I. "Free" Category

1 _____
2 _____
3 _____
4 _____
5 _____

Miracles this week

1 _____
2 _____
3 _____
4 _____
5 _____

Challenges this week

1 _____
2 _____
3 _____
4 _____
5 _____

Additional "to do"

1 _____
2 _____
3 _____
4 _____
5 _____

My successes this week

1 _____
2 _____
3 _____
4 _____
5 _____

Notes

1 _____
2 _____
3 _____
4 _____
5 _____

Extra Projects

1 _____
2 _____
3 _____

4 _____
5 _____

Week 46

From _____ _____
      (Month)   (Day)

To _____ _____
     (Month)   (Day)

A. Home

1 _____
2 _____
3 _____
4 _____
5 _____

B. Health

1 _____
2 _____
3 _____
4 _____
5 _____

C. Personal and Fun

1 _____
2 _____
3 _____
4 _____
5 _____

D. Spiritual

1 _____
2 _____
3 _____
4 _____
5 _____

E. Finance

1 _____
2 _____
3 _____
4 _____
5 _____

F. Friends and Family

1 _____
2 _____
3 _____
4 _____
5 _____

G. Business

1 _____
2 _____
3 _____
4 _____
5 _____

H. Moving On

1 _____
2 _____
3 _____
4 _____
5 _____

I. "Free" Category

1 _____
2 _____
3 _____
4 _____
5 _____

Miracles this week

1 _____
2 _____
3 _____
4 _____
5 _____

Challenges this week

1 _____
2 _____
3 _____
4 _____
5 _____

Additional "to do"

1 _____
2 _____
3 _____
4 _____
5 _____

My successes this week

1 _____
2 _____
3 _____
4 _____
5 _____

Notes

1 _____
2 _____
3 _____
4 _____
5 _____

Extra Projects

1 _____
2 _____
3 _____

4 _____
5 _____

Week 47

From

_____ _____
(Month)   (Day)

To

_____ _____
(Month)   (Day)

A. Home

1 _____
2 _____
3 _____
4 _____
5 _____

B. Health

1 _____
2 _____
3 _____
4 _____
5 _____

C. Personal and Fun

1 _____
2 _____
3 _____
4 _____
5 _____

D. Spiritual

1 _____
2 _____
3 _____
4 _____
5 _____

E. Finance

1 _____
2 _____
3 _____
4 _____
5 _____

F. Friends and Family

1 _____
2 _____
3 _____
4 _____
5 _____

G. Business

1 _____
2 _____
3 _____
4 _____
5 _____

H. Moving On

1 _____
2 _____
3 _____
4 _____
5 _____

I. "Free" Category

1 _____
2 _____
3 _____
4 _____
5 _____

Challenges this week

1 _____
2 _____
3 _____
4 _____
5 _____

My successes this week

1 _____
2 _____
3 _____
4 _____
5 _____

Miracles this week

1 _____
2 _____
3 _____
4 _____
5 _____

Additional "to do"

1 _____
2 _____
3 _____
4 _____
5 _____

Notes

1 _____
2 _____
3 _____
4 _____
5 _____

Extra Projects

1 _____
2 _____
3 _____
4 _____
5 _____

Week 48

From _____ _____
        (Month)   (Day)

To _____ _____
        (Month)   (Day)

A. Home

1 _____
2 _____
3 _____
4 _____
5 _____

B. Health

1 _____
2 _____
3 _____
4 _____
5 _____

C. Personal and Fun

1 _____
2 _____
3 _____
4 _____
5 _____

D. Spiritual

1 _____
2 _____
3 _____
4 _____
5 _____

E. Finance

1 _____
2 _____
3 _____
4 _____
5 _____

F. Friends and Family

1 _____
2 _____
3 _____
4 _____
5 _____

G. Business

1 _____
2 _____
3 _____
4 _____
5 _____

H. Moving On

1 _____
2 _____
3 _____
4 _____
5 _____

I. "Free" Category

1 _____
2 _____
3 _____
4 _____
5 _____

Miracles this week

1 _____
2 _____
3 _____
4 _____
5 _____

Challenges this week

1 _____
2 _____
3 _____
4 _____
5 _____

Additional "to do"

1 _____
2 _____
3 _____
4 _____
5 _____

My successes this week

1 _____
2 _____
3 _____
4 _____
5 _____

Notes

1 _____
2 _____
3 _____
4 _____
5 _____

Extra Projects

1 _____
2 _____
3 _____

4 _____
5 _____

Week 49

From
_____ _____
(Month)   (Day)

To
_____ _____
(Month)   (Day)

A. Home

1 _____
2 _____
3 _____
4 _____
5 _____

B. Health

1 _____
2 _____
3 _____
4 _____
5 _____

C. Personal and Fun

1 _____
2 _____
3 _____
4 _____
5 _____

D. Spiritual

1 _____
2 _____
3 _____
4 _____
5 _____

E. Finance

1 _____
2 _____
3 _____
4 _____
5 _____

F. Friends and Family

1 _____
2 _____
3 _____
4 _____
5 _____

G. Business

1 _____
2 _____
3 _____
4 _____
5 _____

H. Moving On

1 _____
2 _____
3 _____
4 _____
5 _____

I. "Free" Category

1 _____
2 _____
3 _____
4 _____
5 _____

Miracles this week

1 _____
2 _____
3 _____
4 _____
5 _____

Challenges this week

1 _____
2 _____
3 _____
4 _____
5 _____

Additional "to do"

1 _____
2 _____
3 _____
4 _____
5 _____

My successes this week

1 _____
2 _____
3 _____
4 _____
5 _____

Notes

1 _____
2 _____
3 _____
4 _____
5 _____

Extra Projects

1 _____
2 _____
3 _____

4 _____
5 _____

Week 50   From _____ _____   To _____ _____

(Month)   (Day)   (Month)   (Day)

A. Home

1 _____
2 _____
3 _____
4 _____
5 _____

B. Health

1 _____
2 _____
3 _____
4 _____
5 _____

C. Personal and Fun

1 _____
2 _____
3 _____
4 _____
5 _____

D. Spiritual

1 _____
2 _____
3 _____
4 _____
5 _____

E. Finance

1 _____
2 _____
3 _____
4 _____
5 _____

F. Friends and Family

1 _____
2 _____
3 _____
4 _____
5 _____

G. Business

1 _____
2 _____
3 _____
4 _____
5 _____

H. Moving On

1 _____
2 _____
3 _____
4 _____
5 _____

I. "Free" Category

1 _____
2 _____
3 _____
4 _____
5 _____

Challenges this week

1 _____
2 _____
3 _____
4 _____
5 _____

My successes this week

1 _____
2 _____
3 _____
4 _____
5 _____

Miracles this week

1 _____
2 _____
3 _____
4 _____
5 _____

Additional "to do"

1 _____
2 _____
3 _____
4 _____
5 _____

Notes

1 _____
2 _____
3 _____
4 _____
5 _____

Extra Projects

1 _____
2 _____
3 _____

4 _____
5 _____

Week 51

From
_____ _____
(Month)   (Day)

To
_____ _____
(Month)   (Day)

A. Home

1 _____
2 _____
3 _____
4 _____
5 _____

B. Health

1 _____
2 _____
3 _____
4 _____
5 _____

C. Personal and Fun

1 _____
2 _____
3 _____
4 _____
5 _____

D. Spiritual

1 _____
2 _____
3 _____
4 _____
5 _____

E. Finance

1 _____
2 _____
3 _____
4 _____
5 _____

F. Friends and Family

1 _____
2 _____
3 _____
4 _____
5 _____

G. Business

1 _____
2 _____
3 _____
4 _____
5 _____

H. Moving On

1 _____
2 _____
3 _____
4 _____
5 _____

I. "Free" Category

1 _____
2 _____
3 _____
4 _____
5 _____

Miracles this week

1 _____
2 _____
3 _____
4 _____
5 _____

Challenges this week

1 _____
2 _____
3 _____
4 _____
5 _____

Additional "to do"

1 _____
2 _____
3 _____
4 _____
5 _____

My successes this week

1 _____
2 _____
3 _____
4 _____
5 _____

Notes

1 _____
2 _____
3 _____
4 _____
5 _____

Extra Projects

1 _____
2 _____
3 _____

4 _____
5 _____

Week 52　From　_____　_____　To　_____　_____
　　　　　　(Month)　　　　　　(Day)　　　　　　(Month)　　　　　　(Day)

A. Home

1 _____
2 _____
3 _____
4 _____
5 _____

B. Health

1 _____
2 _____
3 _____
4 _____
5 _____

C. Personal and Fun

1 _____
2 _____
3 _____
4 _____
5 _____

D. Spiritual

1 _____
2 _____
3 _____
4 _____
5 _____

E. Finance

1 _____
2 _____
3 _____
4 _____
5 _____

F. Friends and Family

1 _____
2 _____
3 _____
4 _____
5 _____

G. Business

1 _____
2 _____
3 _____
4 _____
5 _____

H. Moving On

1 _____
2 _____
3 _____
4 _____
5 _____

I. "Free" Category

1 _____
2 _____
3 _____
4 _____
5 _____

Challenges this week

1 _____
2 _____
3 _____
4 _____
5 _____

My successes this week

1 _____
2 _____
3 _____
4 _____
5 _____

Miracles this week

1 _____
2 _____
3 _____
4 _____
5 _____

Additional "to do"

1 _____
2 _____
3 _____
4 _____
5 _____

Notes

1 _____
2 _____
3 _____
4 _____
5 _____

Extra Projects

1 _____
2 _____
3 _____

4 _____
5 _____

$\mathcal{L}$ife is not measured by the number of breaths we take, but by the moments that take our breath away.

—Maya Angelou

Your Year End Review (52 Weeks)

*T*his is great!

   You have accomplished fifty-two weeks of Perfect Planning 4 Life! A complete year!

1) Grab your partner and make a date to review your completed categories.

2) Have both of your "PP4Life" workbooks ready and marked. Please notice what has been completed, what are the struggles, and what needs to be looked at that you may be avoiding. All this is very revealing.

3) Open your workbook to the Master Categories Chart and write in the number of goals that you completed for the year! This is *your* wrap-up!

4) You may also want to pencil in the percentage of what you have accomplished, and this will give you an idea of if you are on schedule for the year or if you really have to start to focus on what you have not accomplished and why.

5) *Do not* be discouraged! Celebrate what you have accomplished and look at the items that are not accomplished:
   A. Is the timing off?
   B. Was it too aggressive?
   C. Will you be able to complete this goal later in the following year?
   D. Be honest with yourself… This is how you grow!

When you look at what you have accomplished, *please* celebrate that victory!

When you start the next year, hold on to this workbook and "roll over" anything that needs to be addressed. That's okay.

Be proud of yourself.

Feel blessed and move forward.

You are an amazing person.

Now get another *Perfect Planning 4 Life!* workbook, and let's start your journey of success again! Please visit my website at any time to get more ideas: www.perfectplanning4life.com.

I wish you great joy and success in your life!

Year Wrap Up Summary

Year Wrap Up Summary

Items Complete for the Year

52 Weeks of

From

_____ _____
(Month)   (Day)

To

_____ _____
(Month)   (Day)

A. Home

1 _____
2 _____
3 _____
4 _____
5 _____

B. Health

1 _____
2 _____
3 _____
4 _____
5 _____

C. Personal and Fun

1 _____
2 _____
3 _____
4 _____
5 _____

D. Spiritual

1 _____
2 _____
3 _____
4 _____
5 _____

E. Finance

1 _____
2 _____
3 _____
4 _____
5 _____

F. Friends and Family

1 _____
2 _____
3 _____
4 _____
5 _____

G. Business

1 _____
2 _____
3 _____
4 _____
5 _____

H. Moving On

1 _____
2 _____
3 _____
4 _____
5 _____

Think of what you have accomplished! Look at what you may want to roll over to the next year.

I. "Free" Category

1 _____
2 _____
3 _____
4 _____
5 _____

Miracles this week

1 _____
2 _____
3 _____
4 _____
5 _____

Challenges this year

1 _____
2 _____
3 _____
4 _____
5 _____

Additional "to do"

1 _____
2 _____
3 _____
4 _____
5 _____

My successes this year

1 _____
2 _____
3 _____
4 _____
5 _____

Notes

1 _____
2 _____
3 _____
4 _____
5 _____

Extra Projects

1 _____
2 _____
3 _____

4 _____
5 _____

Additional Notes and Thoughts

Week From _____ To _____ _____
(Month)   (Day)   (Month)   (Day)

Home

1 _____
2 _____
3 _____
4 _____
5 _____

Health

1 _____
2 _____
3 _____
4 _____
5 _____

Personal and Fun

1 _____
2 _____
3 _____
4 _____
5 _____

Spiritual

1 _____
2 _____
3 _____
4 _____
5 _____

Finance

1 _____
2 _____
3 _____
4 _____
5 _____

Friends and Family

1 _____
2 _____
3 _____
4 _____
5 _____

Business

1 _____
2 _____
3 _____
4 _____
5 _____

Moving On

1 _____
2 _____
3 _____
4 _____
5 _____

Notes, Thoughts, and Journals

1 _____

2 _____

3 _____

4 _____

5 _____

6 _____

7 _____

8 _____

9 _____

10 _____

11 _____

12 _____

13 _____

14 _____

15 _____

16 _____

17 _____

18 _____

19 _____

20 _____

Tina Russek was organized in her mother's womb. It was in her DNA. All her life, Tina organized her clothes, accessories, living space, and workplace. To her it was simply an easier and more efficient way to live.

"You can't use it if you can't see it," and "Clean up, clean out, save space" were her mantras. It all worked for Tina Russek as she organized, designed, and built her client's closets and offices, which became *A Perfect Closet 4 You!*

As time went by, Tina realized that time itself needed to be organized.

Time management was a new frontier that needed to be addressed and embraced, harnessed, and planned; thus, *Perfect Planning 4 Life* was born.

Clients that loved Tina's custom designed closets and office systems were now asking about her time management and how has she accomplished so much in her day-to-day life.

Enter *Perfect Planning 4 Life: The Workbook* A very friendly fifty-two-week, fill-in-the-blank, yearly tool that will help the readers organize all the goals they wish to accomplish every year.

This fabulous workbook will guide you through the breakdown and process of determining the goals you want to achieve every year of your life. The workbook also serves as a record of your successes and challenges as you navigate your journey.

All in all, this is a book that will help you organize and accomplish all the things you want to do in fifty-two weeks, one day at a time!

All you have to do is…fill in the blank!

CPSIA information can be obtained
at www.ICGtesting.com
Printed in the USA
LVHW060014280122
709435LV00015B/623

9 781662 436987